PUBLIC SPEAKING MADE EASY

START OFF STRONG, END POWERFUL, AND HAVE FUN IN THE PROCESS

DANIEL ROBBINS

CONTENTS

Introduction   v

1. What Is Public Speaking?   1
2. The Importance of Public Speaking   5
3. Public Speaking Challenges   8
4. Making The First 90 Seconds Count   10
5. Story-Telling   12
6. Adding Humor To Your Speech   15
7. Reading The Audience   19

Afterword   23

INTRODUCTION

We will dive into the following topics and create a step-by-step method for creating highly effective speeches. This will be easy to follow, entertaining to read, and use examples from real speeches.

Some of the topics covered include:

- Creating an opener that instantly hooks
    - Keeping your listeners on the edge of their seats
    - How to create enticing stories
    - How to bring characters to life
    - Making your story visually intriguing – like a movie
    - Speeches that the audience will remember for years
    - Forming the speech to match the audience
    - Strategies to add humor to the stories
    - Methods to create smooth topic shifts so that it flows
    - Tips to create analogies or metaphors
    - Ways to build rapport with the audience
    - Vocal tonality and range to keep listeners excited
    - How to creatively summarize the main points

1
WHAT IS PUBLIC SPEAKING?

Rhetoric is the art of ruling the minds of men. –Plato

Identifying the origins of public speaking will lead one to the written treatises of the ancient Greeks 2500 years ago. Although most books attribute the beginning of public speaking to the Greeks, it must be understood that the art of public speaking was practiced even long before this era. In fact the oldest known handbook that talks about effective speech was written 4500 years ago on papyrus in Ancient Egypt. The Greeks, however, were the first ones to master the art of public speaking; thus, people attribute the said field of communication to the Greeks. For the Greeks, public speaking, which they referred to as "rhetoric," is not just a form of communication but a way of life (DeCaro).

Understanding public speaking will require a person to understand how it started, at least from the point of view of written records. Going back to the early Greek times will be a good starting point for a journey headed to a holistic understanding of public speaking.

As mentioned earlier, rhetoric was the term used by

Greeks to refer to the art of public speaking. This played a pivotal role in the lives of the Greeks and the Romans later on. Aristotle defined rhetoric as the "faculty of discovering in the particular case all the available means of persuasion" (Kennedy, 1963). Indeed, for the Greeks, public speaking was the primary means to persuade other people regarding a specific matter. Its importance in education and civic life was undeniable during this era. For the Greek civilization, oral expression was significant.

The birth of democracy in Greece highlighted the people's need for public speaking. The reign of Pericles (461 BC to 429 BC) brought pure democracy to the society. With the liberalized judicial system, even the poor were given the right to be included in the process henceforth serving juries. Moreover, the leadership of Pericles made it possible for any Athenian to oppose and propose laws during assembly. These changes in the political system of the society made more people involved in public speaking. Thus, everyone who wanted to be heard must have the skills necessary to make the rest of the crowd listen (DeCaro).

The reason why early Greeks are most often identified with the concept of public speaking is the nature of their society that is free. Persuasion is powerful in a free society. Every individual, given the right to dip into political and governmental policies, would always want to change some aspects of the immediate reality. In such a society, the better that one is in persuading, the more influential he/she gets. Persuasive public speaking and democracy are inseparable.

· · ·

ATHENIANS REALIZED that their future depended largely on their ability to speak persuasively (Murphy and Katula, 1995). The juries of Pericles numbered from 500 to 1000; thus, for a person to speak in a legislative assembly, he or she required a highly developed and polished debate. A person must be able to display outstanding public speaking skills to be worthy of the juries' attention and time. What were debated in such public meetings is of utmost importance for the Greeks; they involve issues that can define peace and/or war for the entire society (DeCaro).

IT IS NOT BY MUSCLE, speed or physical dexterity that great things are achieved, but by reflection, force of character and judgment.
–Marcus Tullius Cicero

ROMAN RHETORIC, on the other hand, appeared in the second century BC. At first, the teachers of rhetoric in Rome were Greeks but later on Roman teachers were produced. How rhetoric was developed and completed in the Roman times is not entirely clear; nonetheless, two famous personalities who are still widely known nowadays are products of the Roman rhetoric—Cicero and Quintilian.

Among the contributions of Cicero in the field of public speaking is the notion that the orator must possess a firm foundation of general knowledge. Being conversant is a trait that Cicero believes to be a requirement for a person to be an effective speaker. Moreover, a person must possess a wide range of information/knowledge. Cicero considers orators who largely depend on elegant words and perfect diction but lack substance to be shallow speakers. For him, rhetoric must be used to mold public opinion.

Quintilian was born a hundred years after Cicero's death; thus, a lot has changed in the realm of education and rhetoric. Quintilian adopted Cicero's concise style for his advocacy for rhetoric to return to clearer and simpler language. During Quintilian's time, what became popular was the use of excessive ornamentation in the oratory style and he totally disliked it. According to him, this contributed only to further confusion between the listener and the speaker.

Rhetoric continued to be valued through the middle ages, and during the Renaissance period, there was a rebirth of the Greek and Roman traditional perception of public speaking. Moreover, in this age of "enlightenment," humanist and rationalist thinkers emerged. In the late 18th and early 19th centuries, public speaking was used, for a short period of time, as a means of entertainment.

Today, public speaking has adopted yet another innovation brought about by the modern time and context. The face-to-face communication is just one among the many media one can use to reach and influence the public. The Internet, radio, television and print are just among the several multimedia commonly used by speakers to give the masses their message. Although public speaking seems to carry different hues depending on the social and temporal context, the concept itself basically remained the same. Nonetheless, how one era views and understands public speaking varies.

2

THE IMPORTANCE OF PUBLIC SPEAKING

Speech is the mirror of action. –Solon

Public speaking, as the name suggests, talks about making one's ideas public. The pivotal role played by public speaking never faltered through time. Until now, sharing one's ideas, philosophies and information to touch and somehow influence other people's minds is significant in several aspects of human life.

Several personalities were able to influence almost the entire world through their public speaking. These personalities include Franklin Roosevelt, British Prime Minister Margaret Thatcher, South African leader Nelson Mandela, Ronald Reagan, Martin Luther King, Jr., Hillary Clinton, and Barack Obama. Although all of the names mentioned are the big names in their respective fields, public speaking is not a skill exclusive to the rich and the famous. Everyone, at some point in their lives, will need to stand up in front of several people and deliver a talk or speech.

THERE ARE several professions that would require one to

consistently carry out a public speech from time to time. Teachers/professors, lawyers, scientists, public relations officers, engineers, health care officers, and advertising officers belong to the communication profession category of the contemporary. These professions require an individual to develop outstanding communication skills, which must include public speaking skills, to be able to effectively perform his/her job.

PUBLIC SPEAKING, however, is not just limited to the communication professions. Today, the ability to speak effectively is among the qualities companies from different industries are looking for. Job applicants are now asked to give a presentation as part of their job interview. Significantly, companies who are using such activity to assess applicants are growing in numbers. This shows that the corporate world is in need of employees who are not just equipped with the knowledge and technical know-how but also public speaking skills.

THE IMPORTANCE of public speaking skills goes beyond one's professional life; it also matters most in one's civic engagements. For a person who carries ideologies, beliefs and ideas regarding global issues that significantly matter, having the ability to speak in public is of utmost importance. Some people care so much about something that they want to make a difference. For instance, a person is concerned with the environmental problems the world is experiencing and he/she wants other people to see through his/her lens so they could see things like how he/she does; then carrying out a public speech could give him/her the best platform to achieve the goal of making a difference.

PUBLIC SPEAKING IS important in persuading other people. Just like how the Greeks saw it thousands of years ago, having the ability to persuade will give one the opportunity to influence important areas of the society's functioning and the areas in their personal lives as well. Public speaking is important to get listeners to agree with the perspective presented; thus if one's goal is to defend an idea, sell a program, counter an opponent and inspire people to take action, then public speaking skills are necessary.

EVEN IN THE EVERYDAY EXPERIENCE, a person will definitely encounter a reason to deliver a speech in front of a crowd. It may be in the form of a school activity, or a job-related presentation or an invitation from a social organization. Whatever the form or nature of the reason behind the need to perform public speaking, one must keep in mind that what matters is not the volume or the importance of the information the person is going to give, not the numbers of jargon or hifalutin words used but how he/she affects the audience.

3
PUBLIC SPEAKING CHALLENGES

Public speaking skills can be learned by anyone. Although charisma can be considered a gift to some people, being able to communicate with the audience accordingly can definitely be practiced and mastered through time.

Some people, however, experience difficulty in delivering their speech in front of a crowd, basically because of anxiety or stage fright. Shaking of the hands, sweaty palms and drying of the mouth are just some of the things experienced by a person when under the pressure of giving a speech in front of a big audience. Feeling anxious or nervous before and during the presentation will definitely affect the outcome of the event. The effectiveness of public speaking in influencing the lives and minds of other people might not be maximized if the speaker himself will be troubled by his/her fear of the stage. Fortunately there are ways on how to eliminate the fear or anxiety of a person in public speaking.

Practice is important to eliminate emotional distractions like fear or anxiety. One may practice in front of the mirror or in front of friends and/or family. By practicing, one is enabling oneself to master not just the words to be spoken, but also the gestures, tone of the voice and facial expressions necessary to make the speech more effective. A person who is confident that he/she knows exactly what to say and what to do in front of the audience will definitely have lesser fear or anxiety with public speaking.

Visiting the venue prior the speech will definitely help one feel more comfortable with the setting itself. Familiarizing oneself with the location of the lighting, the prompter, the arrangement of the seat for audiences and the position of the monitor (for visual presentations) will add more confidence to the speaker. Knowing how to maneuver the materials available and utilize the facility itself will make the speaker look experienced and well rehearsed.

Before the presentation, one can try doing relaxing activities. Allotting a couple of minutes for a short meditation, stretching and walking, listening to favorite music or reading motivational quotes can help one release a good amount of pressure or anxiety.

If the speaker is a non-coffee drinker, then he/she must not drink coffee or any caffeinated drink before the speech. The said drink will not serve as an energy booster; rather it can cause a faster heart rate and more anxiety for the speaker. However, for coffee drinkers, consuming his/her daily cup is advisable. Some coffee drinkers are not comfortable without having at least a sip of their preferred drink. Thus, if having a cup or two will make him/her feel and perform better, then he/she must not forget about it.

During the presentation, making eye contact with the audience will help remove the anxiety or fear felt. When one is looking at another person's eye during a presentation, the feeling of "just conversing" might occur and this will make the speaker relaxed and more spontaneous during the speech. Moreover, eye contact will make a person less isolated and more involved with the audience - making him/her more comfortable in delivering the presentation.

These are just some of the things one can try to remove the anxiety or fear in speaking in public. Research shows that people deliver speeches at least once in their lives; thus, knowing how to deal with it with flying colors is of utmost importance.

An effective speaker, however, takes more than a person having little or no public speaking anxiety at all. There are several other important factors that must be considered in the process. Public speaking is more than standing before a crowd while uttering words. The speaker must always be able to reach the audience and to influence them. A successful speech is the one that people remember.

So, how one can make a speech of a lifetime?

4

MAKING THE FIRST 90 SECONDS COUNT

If there is a moment that people are most receptive, that would be the very first 60-90 seconds of the speech. The beginning of public speaking is very crucial in the relationship between the audience and the speaker. This is the reason why the opening part must not be wasted; rather it must be utilized to immediately engage the audience in the speech. The problem however is that some speakers need some time to get comfortable with the stage while some use the very first minute to thank several people.

The speaker must always take advantage of the beginning of the speech to build a connection with the audience immediately. Starting with the self-introduction or with the title of the presentation might not be the best way to utilize the first 60-90 seconds of the time. Creating an opener that instantly hooks the audience does not require a genius out of the speaker; one just needs to ignite the audience's "need to know" (Doree, 2008).

The most effective ways to immediately engage the audience includes stating startling statistics. Shocking the audience with facts and figures that they don't normally hear about will definitely make them want to know more.

Opening with a question is also another effective way to grab the audience's attention. Basically a conversation starts with a question and that is just what is happening when a speaker asks the audience a question. By doing so, the speaker is involving the crowd in the process already. By using a question to start the speech, the speaker is, in a way, telling the audience that "This event is not just about me." Bringing the audience in an enlarged conversation will definitely make them listen.

One could also start with a challenge or a provocative question. Making people think from the beginning will make them want to follow the flow of details of the speech all throughout. Audiences attending speeches are most likely active listeners. Making them think will not make them walk away rather it would keep them in their seats. If the speaker has a goal in mind, so does every individual in the audience seat. They attend such events because they wanted information, education, inspiration or just something to think about. If a person wanted just pure entertainment without the need to rack his brain about a challenge or a puzzle, then he/she would rather go see a movie than listen to a speaker. Thus, a speaker must not hesitate to throw challenges and questions to his/her spectators.

5
STORY-TELLING

What's interesting about the human brain is that it cannot easily remember facts as it can remember stories. If one is asked about the stories his/her parents told him/her during childhood, one can definitely provide several. A story is always interesting for a person. Perhaps the brain is wired to follow through the events where something is happening to a protagonist. Once a person is exposed to the beginning of a story, the curiosity of how it will end is immediately triggered; thus he/she will keep on listening until he learns what happened in the end.

The magic brought about by story-telling to audiences can definitely help speakers to catch the listeners' attention as well as to keep them on the edge of their seats. Incorporating stories in speeches to make them more appealing to audiences is a technique utilized by several renowned speakers. One of the speakers who creatively and successfully used story telling in her public speaking is two-time Nobel Prize winner and the person responsible in the discovery of radium, Marie Curie.

In her speech to inspire the graduating class of 1921, Marie Curie talked about radium through storytelling. Here is how she started her speech:

"Radium is no more a baby, it is more than 20 years old, but the conditions of the discovery were somewhat peculiar, and so it is always of interest to remember them and to explain them."

Marie Curie was aware that she was talking to a group of people from different fields of expertise so not all are well-versed in the scientific jargons and contention; thus, Curie used story-telling incorporating scientific facts to be able to make everyone follow her discussion.

Just like how Marie Curie utilized story-telling to capture her audience's attention, everyone can be creative enough to create a jump-start out of stories in speeches. What's important to keep in mind in using this technique is to understand the diversity of the audience. Once identified, one can decide on the kind of story that would definitely relate to the experiences of the spectators. The more they can relate to the events happening to the protagonist, the deeper is the connection happening between them and the speaker. This is one way to make stories enticing for the listeners.

The stories incorporated in speeches must give the listeners the creative preview of what is to follow. To make it more enticing there must be some unexpected twists that the crowd would not anticipate. Stories of quests, love and rags to riches are commonly used primarily because their appeal to the audiences across culture and time never fades.

To make stories more enticing and effective, one must be

able to vividly describe the characters of the story. Giving explicit descriptions will help the audience visualize the characters, thus making the characters come alive in the listeners' minds. Coupling story telling with visual presentation, for instance, a slide show of pictures can help make the story more visually intriguing for the audience.

For more information on storytelling strategies and tips, I highly recommend The Storytelling Method by Matt Morris. It talks about 10-steps to telling an inspirational and unforgettable story!

6
ADDING HUMOR TO YOUR SPEECH

Dying is easy. Comedy is hard. – Meryl Streep
One of the best ways on how to make an impact on other people's lives is perhaps, making them laugh. A shared laughter is rarely forgotten. Possibly among the very first things that are popping in a speaker's mind when caught in front of a crowd is how to make everyone lighten up through laughter. Nonetheless, the use of comedy in speech can be a dangerous act. What's funny can be relative. A joke can make a particular group of people laugh out loud but could be offensive for others. The crowd is never a homogenous one. There is always going to be different groups of people in the audience; thus, when one plans to use jokes or satirical stories to stimulate a relaxed atmosphere, it must be done with utmost consideration.

Although humor in speech is a delicate move, it is commonly used even in serious settings for formal speeches. A good laugh shared by the audience can give a positive perspective for both the listener and the speaker. Moreover, nothing beats laughter in unifying the audience.

Will Rogers is considered a master of using comedy to make the audience concentrate on the message of his speech. He was first a stand-up comedian, which explains why he is very good at making people laugh, and later on became popular in the film industry. Below is an excerpt coming from Rogers' speech in Columbia University in 1924;

> "President Butler paid me a compliment in mentioning my name
> in his introductory remarks this evening. ... I am glad he did that,
> because I got the worst of it last week. The Prince of Wales, in
> speaking of the sights of America, mentioned the Woolworth
> Building, the subway, the slaughterhouse, Will Rogers, and the
> Ford factory. He could at least put me ahead of the hogs."

A SPEAKER DOES NEED NOT to be a stand-up comedian first before he/she can effectively include humor in his/her speech like Rogers. Humor is a great tool to make one's speech memorable and more powerful. Luckily, delivering a joke to tickle a crowd can be considered a skill that can be enhanced.

The crucial aspects of presenting a joke in front of spectators include timing and delivery. Even if a person is cracking the funniest joke ever, it will not be successful without the perfect combination of how to say it and when to hit the words and when to pause. This is the reason why two people can tell the same joke to the same audience and gather different responses.

Even in trying to be funny, practice is important. Although for other people, being a comedian comes naturally, others need to master it through practice and hard work. It is said that even the great materials in the field of comedy that sounds impromptu, are well-rehearsed prior the event.

One may start with practicing through voice recording it. Listening to the recorded voice will allow one to analyze how he/she delivers the joke. This way, one can adjust pauses to where they work best. Making a joke sound like it is not rehearsed can also be achieved through practice.

Humor never fails in almost all the areas of human life. People become more engaged with the speech when the speaker can make them laugh for a moment. Nonetheless, one must keep in mind that the use of humor must highlight the theme or topic of the speech. It must not serve as a distraction for the audience. It is an effective tool that must be used to keep the audience on their seats involved and not to disengage them from a serious matter. Humor incorporated in speech must also reflect the personality of the speaker.

How To Have Your Voice Work For You

A GREAT CONTRAST always arouses attention. - Dale Carnegie (Carnegie & Esenwein, 1915)

Emphasis is important in a speech. The audience, among the thousands of words mentioned, must be able to retain words that were given appropriate emphasis.

Through changing the voice's pitches, one can keep the audience listening all throughout the discussion. A speaker must be able to use the power of contrast to make sure that the listeners will not miss all the important points mentioned. Sudden shifts from high to low pitch, and vice versa, will definitely catch a person's attention for it is making the statement more interesting and intriguing.

Another way to make the audience more active in listening is through having variations in speaking. This is done by avoiding the cardinal sin of speaker, which is speaking in a monotonous manner. A monotonous speaker uses the same volume, pitch of the tone, emphasis, thoughts and speed. The words have the tendency to sound the same to a listener if they are spoken in a monotonous way. The words normally have power but they end up meaningless if they are not given life through speaking.

One can avoid presenting his/her speech in a monotonous manner by assessing every statement included in the speech. In every statement there are words that must be given more emphasis than their neighboring words. The speaker can easily identify the words to stress when his/her goal for making the speech is crystal clear to him/her.

Through adjusting the volume of the voice, one is not just stressing important words, but also giving more power and conviction to the message itself. Delivering a memorized speech increases the likelihood of the speech being presented in a monotonous way. Hence, practicing the changes in volume, tone and speed as one is presenting the speech is definitely a good idea.

Boredom and weariness are the words directly associated with a monotonous speaker; thus, if there is one thing that a speaker must avoid first and foremost, it would definitely be a single-toned kind of presentation.

7
READING THE AUDIENCE

Reading The Audience
A speaker is offering his/her speech to a crowd and this crowd of listeners is very important in the event. With public speaking, the speaker is aiming at influencing the people's minds and hearts. Thus, it is essential for one to understand his/her audience before coming up with a presentation.

The diversity of the audience is, perhaps, the biggest challenge for a speaker. How he/she involves everyone in a certain topic and a specific point of view will influence the success of the speech. Knowing who will be in the audience will help in assessing the diversity of the crowd. For a very big crowd, it is imperative for the speaker to know the listeners individually. What's important are the general information like the age range of the people, gender, nationality and the like.

A speaker who knows his/her crowd before the speech will definitely be guided in identifying appropriate language, visual presentation and even the kind of humor to use during the presentation.

Also, the audience must feel that the speaker is speaking for them. The speaker must effectively involve and focus on the audience. One must make the crowd feel that the presentation is significant to their lives. Let us see how a renowned speaker, Mahatma Gandhi, focuses on his audience;

"Nonviolence is the first article

of my faith. It is the last article of my faith. But I had to make a

choice. I had either to submit to a system which I considered has

done irreparable harm to my country, or incur the risk of the mad

fury of my people bursting forth when they understood the truth

from my lips.

I HAVE no personal ill-will against any single administrator, much less

can I have any disaffection towards the King's person. But I hold it

to be a virtue to be disaffected towards a government which in its

totality has done more harm to India than any previous system.

I am here, therefore, to invite and submit cheerfully to the highest

penalty that can be inflicted upon me for what in law is a deliberate

crime, and what appear to me to be the highest duty of a citizen."

Building rapport with the audience can be done in

several ways, some of which are mentioned already in the previous pages. Sincerity with the words spoken always connects the speaker to the spectators. This can be achieved by showing genuine concern and presence all throughout the presentation. Verbal and non-verbal cues must go together to be able to convince the crowd of one's sincerity.

Relating the presentation to the audience's experiences will create a bond between the listener and the speaker. This is another way to build rapport with the audience. Once the people can identify with what the speaker is saying, they get to feel more comfortable and attached to the discussion.

Standing in front of the crowd and telling personal stories will also help a speaker connect with the listeners. Some speakers might appear intimidating to some people; thus, a speaker must make the audience see a "commoner" in him/her. By telling stories and experiences that people can definitely relate to, the speaker is allowing the audience to feel a personal connection with him/her.

Sharing a vision with the audience will help a speaker connect with them deeper. To fully understand this, the following excerpt from Martin Luther King Jr.'s very famous speech entitled *I have a Dream* will be of great help:

I have a dream that one day this nation will rise up and live out the

true meaning of its creed [stops his own words and

quotes the Declaration of Independence]: "We hold these truths to

be self-evident, that all men are created equal."

I have a dream that my four little children will one day live in a

nation where they will not be judged by the color of their skin but by the content of their character.

This speech offered by Martin Luther King Jr. is among the speeches that people will remember for several years. To be able to achieve such accomplishments, one must be able to integrate logic, emotions and personal appeal in his/her speech. Having these three appeals working together will definitely help the speaker create an utmost compelling piece.

Other strategies that can be used include repeating words and phrases to mold a vision in the minds of the listeners. Another is by utilizing familiar quotes, analogies and references of some well-known texts. Most importantly keep eye contact with the audience.

How to End a Speech

People usually remember two parts of a speech or a conversation; these are the beginning and the ending. What's in between is, of course, very significant; nonetheless, how the speaker starts and ends the speech will most likely be remembered by the listeners.

A speaker must take advantage of these and be creative with the parting words as well. One way to accomplish this is by creatively summarizing the important points of the discussion. This can be done with the aid of a slideshow of important concepts embedded in interesting photos directly associated with the topic or theme.

Another is through a story. As discussed earlier, people love stories and they tend to remember them for years. Summarizing important points can also be infused with a story. Ending with a quotation, anecdote, metaphor and a question will be as effective as well. Investing in how one will end the talk is worthwhile for last words last.

AFTERWORD

I hope this book was able to guide you and give you strategies for giving successful, powerful, and inspiring speeches.

Good luck with all your future public speaking presentations!

www.ingramcontent.com/pod-product-compliance
Lightning Source LLC
Chambersburg PA
CBHW070038040426
42333CB00040B/1717